My family community

Bobbie Kalman

Crabtree Publishing Company

www.crabtreebooks.com

Created by Bobbie Kalman

Author and Editor-in-Chief
Bobbie Kalman

Educational consultants
Reagan Miller
Elaine Hurst
Joan King

Editors
Reagan Miller
Joan King
Kathy Middleton

Proofreader
Crystal Sikkens

Design
Bobbie Kalman
Katherine Berti

Photo research
Bobbie Kalman

Production coordinator
Katherine Berti

Prepress technician
Katherine Berti

Photographs
Marc Crabtree: p. 17
All other photographs by Shutterstock

Library and Archives Canada Cataloguing in Publication

Kalman, Bobbie, 1947-
    My family community / Bobbie Kalman.

(My world)
Includes index.
ISBN 978-0-7787-9441-7 (bound).--ISBN 978-0-7787-9485-1 (pbk.)

    1. Families--Juvenile literature. I. Title.
II. Series: My world (St. Catharines, Ont.)

HQ744.K34 2010   j306.85   C2009-906101-5

Library of Congress Cataloging-in-Publication Data

Kalman, Bobbie.
    My family community / Bobbie Kalman.
        p. cm. -- (My world)
    Includes index.
    ISBN 978-0-7787-9485-1 (pbk. : alk. paper) -- ISBN 978-0-7787-9441-7
(reinforced library binding : alk. paper)
    1. Families--Juvenile literature. I. Title.

HQ519.K35 2010
306.85--dc22
                                                        2009041220

Crabtree Publishing Company

www.crabtreebooks.com   1-800-387-7650

Printed in Canada / 102021 / MA20210907

Published in Canada
Crabtree Publishing
616 Welland Ave.
St. Catharines, Ontario
L2M 5V6

Published in the United States
Crabtree Publishing
347 Fifth Ave
Suite 1402-145
New York, NY 10016

Published in the United Kingdom
Crabtree Publishing
Maritime House
Basin Road North, Hove
BN41 1WR

Published in Australia
Crabtree Publishing
Unit 3-5
Currumbin Court
Capalaba QLD 4157

What is in this book?

My family is a community

A **community** is a group of people who live together and care for one another.

There are eight people in my family.
Not all families are as big as mine.
How big is your family community?
Who are the people in your family?

We share many things

My parents, grandparents, brother,
and I share a home.

We share rooms and furniture.

We share our garden and swimming pool.

What does your family share?

In summer, we have barbecues in our back yard.
We cook and clean up together.

Caring for one another

Communities look after people.

My family community looks after me.

My parents feed me and buy me clothes.

They take me to the doctor and dentist.

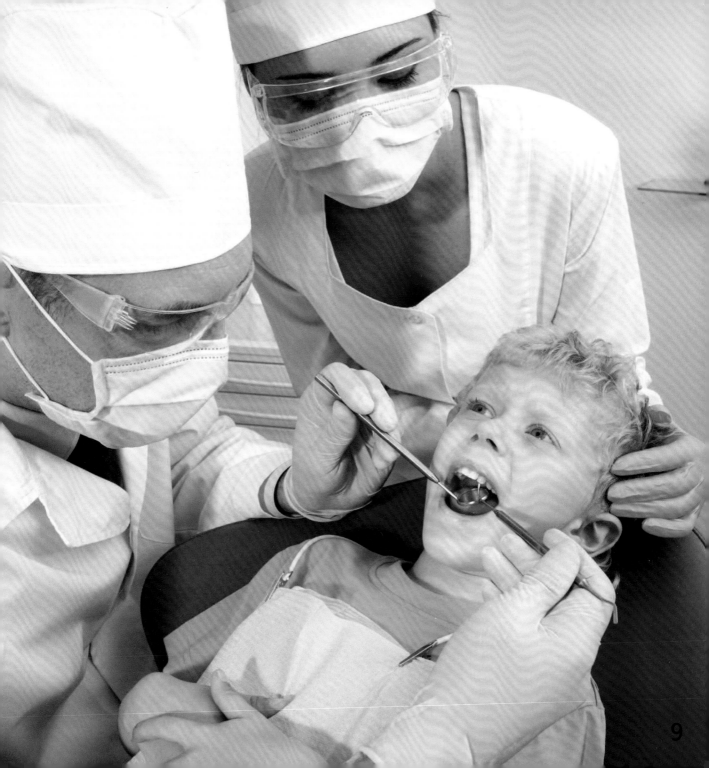

How we travel

People in communities **travel**.

To travel is to go from place to place.

People travel in different ways.

My parents drive to work in our car.

Sometimes I go to school in a school bus.

Sometimes I ride
my bike to school.

Communities teach

Communities have schools,

but my family also teaches me.

My father is teaching me how to play chess.

My mother is teaching me how to paint.

What do you learn from your family?

Working to earn money

My parents work to earn money
to pay for our home and car.
They earn money to pay for food,
clothes, and the other things we need.
My father is a teacher at our school.

My mother is a doctor at a hospital.
Sometimes she works at night.

My rules and jobs

Communities have **laws**, or rules.

I have to follow rules at home, too.

One of the rules is to do my jobs.

I do these jobs to help myself and others.

What are your rules and jobs?

Rules
- Come right home after school
- Go to bed at eight o'clock
- Watch only one hour of television a day
- Be respectful to other people
- Do something kind every day

Jobs

- Do my homework
- Clean my room
- Walk the dog
- Help look after my little sister
- Help with the dishes
- Take out the trash

Family communication

Communication is sharing information.

My family shares information by talking.

We talk to one another about problems.

We share what we did at school.

We talk about our feelings and dreams.

When we are out, we call home to let our family know where we are.

Family history and culture

Communities have **histories**.
Histories are stories about
what happened long ago.
My family has
a history, too.
It also has a **culture**.
Culture is how we live.
It is the food we eat, the clothing
we wear, and the ways we celebrate.
Sometimes we wear special clothes
when we celebrate our culture.

Family fun

Communities are places to have fun.
My family community has a lot of fun!
What fun things does your family do?

We go for
long walks
together.

We sing and dance.

We hug a lot!

We play games.

Words to know and Index